# Powerful
# LEARNING

**Ron Brandt**

Association for Supervision and Curriculum Development
Alexandria, Virginia USA

Association for Supervision and Curriculum Development
1250 N. Pitt Street • Alexandria, Virginia 22314-1453 USA
Telephone: 800-933-2723 or 703-549-9110 • Fax: 703-299-8631
Web site: http://www.ascd.org • E-mail: member@ascd.org

**On July 13, 1998, ASCD will relocate to new headquarters:** 1703 N. Beauregard
St., Alexandria, VA 22311-1714. Telephone: 703-578-9600

Gene R. Carter, *Executive Director*
Michelle Terry, *Assistant Executive
  Director, Program Development*
Nancy Modrak, *Director, Publishing*
John O'Neil, *Acquisitions Editor*
Mark Goldberg, *Development Editor*
Julie Houtz, *Managing Editor of Books*
Kathie Felix, *Associate Editor*
René Bahrenfuss, *Copy Editor*

Deborah Whitley, *Proofreader*
Charles Halverson, *Project Assistant*
Gary Bloom, *Director, Editorial, Design,
  and Production Services*
Karen Monaco, *Senior Designer*
Tracey A. Smith, *Production Manager*
Dina Murray, *Production Coordinator*
John Franklin, *Production Coordinator*
Cindy Stock, *Desktop Publisher*

Printed in the United States of America.                                    S5/98

ASCD Stock No. 198179    ASCD member price: $6.95    nonmember price: $8.95

**Library of Congress Cataloging-in-Publication Data**

Brandt, Ronald S.
  Powerful Learning / Ron Brandt.
      p.   cm.
  Includes bibliographical references (p. ).
  ISBN 0-87120-305-7
    1. Learning, Psychology of.   2. Learning—Social aspects—United States.   3. School
management and organization–United States.
I. Title.
LB1060.B73  1998
370.15'23—dc21

98-17715
CIP

03  02  01  00  99  98      10  9  8  7  6  5  4  3  2  1

# Powerful
# LEARNING

# Preface

Members of the representative group who prepared ASCD's current strategic plan suggested that ASCD publish a statement on learning and distribute it throughout the world. To fulfill that charge, and to help educators clarify their own thoughts about learning, ASCD has produced this book.

*Learning* is an ambiguous term. All forms of animal life—even mealworms—learn; that is, they modify their behavior on the basis of experience. Touching the proverbial hot stove is undeniably a learning experience. So is committing information to memory. In fact, that is what many people mean when they talk of learning. And despite educators' tendency to dismiss "mere rote learning," memorization is an essential skill. Imagine always having to look up the days of the week to see what comes after Tuesday. Actors and musicians routinely demonstrate that memory is more than "mere."

In this book, though, we are referring to more complex learning. Some scholars use the term *productive learning* (Sarason 1997) and others *understanding* (Perkins and Blythe 1994). Caine and Caine (1997) have something similar in mind in their discussion of *dynamical knowledge* (p. 114). No adjective feels just right, but we have chosen to refer to this higher-level learning as *powerful learning.**

---

*Henry Levin's Accelerated Schools Project has emphasized "powerful learning" for some time. Although the term is defined a bit differently in Accelerated Schools, its general meaning is similar to that used here.

# Conditions for Powerful Learning

# Conditions for Powerful Learning

If there is anything educators ought to know about, it is *learning*. We say that students come to school to learn. Our job is to get them to learn. We tell students to "learn this," and we report how well they learned it to parents and policymakers.

We have a general idea what learning is and how it happens. After all, we ourselves have done a lot of learning. And we know some tried and true ways to expedite school learning: give a reading assignment and conduct a recitation, have the student write a paper or solve a make-believe problem, explain something and ask the student to explain it back, or give a test. We use these approaches because we are expected to use them and because they work fairly well.

Much learning takes place in other ways, of course. Young children learn to walk and talk through a natural process of trial and error. Some accomplished artists and musicians are described as self-taught. People solve problems and make scientific discoveries—clearly a form of learning—without being directed by a teacher.

Educators are sometimes intrigued by the contrast between traditional school practices and the way learning takes place in other settings. The respected cognitive researcher Lauren Resnick talked about it in her 1987 presidential address to the American Educational Research Association (Resnick 1987). And before her, generations of teachers undoubtedly looked for ways to somehow make better use of their students' natural learning abilities. Now, with new information from cognitive psychology and brain research, educators have more authoritative knowledge on the subject of learning than ever before.

When I began working on this book I found that several new statements on learning were in preparation or already had been produced. My colleagues at ASCD and I decided not to duplicate these works here, but to build upon them for a slightly different purpose. First, I quote insights about various aspects of learning from three of these documents, revealing an impressive consensus among rather different sources. Next, I propose conditions under which people seem to learn best, also based on the three works. Then I offer examples from recent articles in *Educational Leadership* that I think illustrate how these conditions can be created in schools. Finally, I speculate about how knowledge about learning may apply to organizations as well as to individuals.

The major sources for this book are the newest version of "Learner-Centered Psychological Principles" prepared by a work group of the American Psychological Association (APA), a document called *Teaching for Effective Learning* by the Scottish Consultative Council on the Curriculum (Scottish CCC), and a book by Renate and Geoffrey Caine, *Education on the Edge of Possibility.* I will also mention "Principles of Learning: Challenging Fundamental Assumptions" from the Institute for Research on Learning (IRL), Menlo Park, California. According to these documents, the following can be said about human learning:

**People learn what is personally meaningful to them.** Researchers say that learning is most effective when it is "active, goal-directed," and "personally relevant" (APA 1997). Because "the search for meaning is innate" (Caine and Caine 1997), learners concentrate most on the learning tasks that are personally meaningful to them. Those who want to influence the learning of others should try to create as much correspondence as possible between institutional goals and learners' goals. For example, with the approach called problem-based learning, students acquire valuable knowledge and skills as they investigate real, important problems, such as how to reduce water pollution in a nearby stream.

In other words, people learn when they want to learn. Because "acquisition of complex knowledge and skills requires extended learner effort and guided practice" and because "what and how much is learned is influenced by the learner's motivation" (APA 1997), those who wish to encourage learning must be concerned with what learners feel a need to learn.

Everybody knows the importance of motivation, but teachers are often troubled by the apparent mismatch between student

interests and what the teacher is obliged to teach. Sometimes part of the answer may be found in the way a topic is handled. "Intrinsic motivation is stimulated by tasks of optimal novelty and difficulty" (APA 1997). For example, students may learn about a topic and develop new skills by preparing a report in an unusual way, such as writing a magazine article or producing a video program.

**People learn more when they accept challenging but achievable goals.** Because "there is no limit to growth and to the capacities of humans to learn more" (Caine and Caine 1997), educators must not underestimate what students can do. "We all have much greater potential for learning than is commonly recognized" (Scottish CCC 1996). "Effective learning takes place when learners feel challenged to work toward appropriately high goals" (APA 1997). Learners learn more effectively when teachers demonstrate confidence in their students' abilities and provide "scaffolding" to enable them to perform well on complex tasks. For example, a choral group is more likely to present an outstanding performance when the conductor chooses a technically difficult selection for them to sing, convinces them they can do it, and provides expert coaching.

**Learning is developmental.** Because "there are predetermined sequences of [mental] development in childhood" (Caine and Caine 1997), education is most effective, especially for young children, "when differential development . . . is taken into account" (APA 1997). Similarly, adults who have relatively little experience with a topic (novices) typically approach it differently from those who know more about it (experts). For example, a person with no technical training or experience would probably need more concrete, step-by-step instruction as he learned to make a simple engine repair than someone who had more training and experience but was not familiar with the particular engine involved.

**Individuals learn differently.** Because "every brain is uniquely organized" (Caine and Caine 1997), individuals use "different strategies, approaches, and capabilities," some of which result from "differences in learners' linguistic, cultural, and social backgrounds" (APA 1997). As Howard Gardner contends in his theory of multiple intelligences, "there is no such thing as a single general intelligence" (Scottish CCC 1996). "Self-awareness . . . helps us . . . use our preferred styles . . . to learn more effectively" (Scottish CCC 1996). Schools and other organizations can aid student learning by providing for different ways of learning.

People construct new knowledge by building on their current knowledge. Researchers have found that people learn by "link[ing] new information with existing knowledge in meaningful ways" (APA 1997). Building on what they already know, learners "search for meaning . . . through 'patterning'" (Caine and Caine 1997). Because "learning is messy" (Scottish CCC 1996), an orderly presentation is not necessarily bad, but by itself it may be insufficient. As learners encounter a topic in a variety of ways, they "construct" what they come to know about it.

For example, a person who has attended a class about a new computer program needs to try the program out within a short time. If she has never used a computer but has used a typewriter, she will begin using what she knows about typing, which in some cases will be helpful but in other cases will not. If she has worked with computers before, she will probably be able to use knowledge about them to learn features of the new program more easily. As she uses the program to do a task, she will probably make mistakes and have to correct them. She also may consult an instruction manual or a friend who knows the program. Getting one thing clear at a time, she eventually will become comfortable with the program as a whole—or at least those parts she needs to know.

**Much learning occurs through social interaction.** For years, researchers studied learning as experienced by individual learners, but in recent years they have come to see it as inherently social. In 1992, Gaea Leinhardt called this "the most radical" of all the "new ideas" about learning. "The brain is a social brain" (Caine and Caine 1997), so "most learning involves other people" (Scottish CCC 1996). Because "learning is influenced by social interactions [and] interpersonal relations" (APA 1997), teachers and others who want to promote learning need to pay close attention to the social setting. Students should sometimes work in pairs or learning teams. When teaching the classroom group as a whole, the teacher should strive to develop "a community of inquiry." This means that some teacher-student interaction should go beyond recitation, in which there is a correct answer the teacher expects to hear, and become real discussion, in which students offer conjectures and respond to others' ideas.

The idea that "learning is fundamentally social" is at the heart of a tightly integrated set of principles published by the Institute for Research on Learning (n.d.). The Institute sees learning as "inseparable from engagement in the world." Its seven principles of learning imply that schools should strive to be constellations of small "communities of practice" in which members are continually "negotiating meaning." This idea is elaborated in Etienne Wenger's *Communities of Practice* (1998).

**People need feedback to learn.** One explanation for the power of social interaction is that, among other things, it provides feedback to learners. Feedback—information from outside regarding the accuracy and relevance of our thoughts and actions—is essential to learning. "Ongoing assessment . . . can provide valuable feedback" (APA 1997). "The entire system [body, mind, and brain] interacts with and exchanges information with its environment" (Caine and Caine 1997). This suggests that educators must try to make sure that learners receive accurate, useful, and timely feedback. For example, writers need to know from readers whether their message is clearly understood and, if not, what changes would help.

**Successful learning involves use of strategies—which themselves are learned.** "Learning always involves conscious and unconscious processes" (Caine and Caine 1997), including "thinking and reasoning strategies" (APA 1997). For example,

people frequently "can learn how to learn" by "sharing aims, planning targets, and reviewing achievement" (Scottish CCC 1996). This critical aspect of self-management is sometimes called metacognition or executive control. To help develop it, young people should be coached to think ahead to make sure they have the time and necessary tools for a project and that they have envisioned the steps they will follow to complete it. Then they should be reminded to monitor their own progress as they proceed with the project.

**A positive emotional climate strengthens learning.** Research evidence also suggests that "our ability to think and to learn effectively . . . are closely linked to our physical and emotional well being" (Scottish CCC 1996). "Motivation to learn . . . is influenced by the individual's emotional states" (APA 1997). Thus "an appropriate emotional climate is indispensable to sound education" (Caine and Caine 1997). The relationship between emotions and learning is complex. Strong emotions actually enhance memory, but in general, people learn poorly in stressful environments—and schools by their very nature can be stressful. Schools and other organizations can foster learning by stimulating positive emotions: curiosity, excitement, laughter, enjoyment, and appreciation.

**Learning is influenced by the total environment.** Because "learning involves both focused attention and peripheral perception" (Caine and Caine 1997), it "is influenced by environmental factors" (APA 1997). This means that educators need to attend to all aspects of the setting—physical, social, and

---

**Figure 1**

## SUMMARY STATEMENTS ABOUT LEARNING

1. People learn what is personally meaningful to them.

2. People learn when they accept challenging but achievable goals.

3. Learning is developmental.

4. Individuals learn differently.

5. People construct new knowledge by building on their current knowledge.

6. Much learning occurs through social interaction.

7. People need feedback to learn.

8. Successful learning involves use of strategies—which themselves are learned.

9. A positive emotional climate strengthens learning.

10. Learning is influenced by the total environment.

---

psychological— where learning is supposed to take place. For example, students are probably more likely to remember a play if they act it out, complete with simple costumes, than if they only read it.

These general principles summarizing what is known about how people learn (Figure 1) suggest conditions under which

---

### Figure 2

---

## CONDITIONS FOR POWERFUL LEARNING

In general, we can say that people learn well under the following conditions:

### What They Learn

1. What they learn is personally meaningful.

2. What they learn is challenging and they accept the challenge.

3. What they learn is appropriate for their developmental level.

### How They Learn

4. They can learn in their own way, have choices, and feel in control.

5. They use what they already know as they construct new knowledge.

6. They have opportunities for social interaction.

7. They get helpful feedback.

8. They acquire and use strategies.

### Where They Learn

9. They experience a positive emotional climate.

10. The environment supports the intended learning.

---

students will learn especially well. These conditions are summarized in Figure 2. They encompass the knowledge and skills students are expected to learn, how they go about learning, and the setting in which the learning takes place.

# Powerful Learning in Schools

# Powerful Learning in Schools

By themselves, these guidelines are probably too abstract to be very helpful. To make such statements useful, educators need to think about them; elaborate them; and apply them to their own circumstances, making them personally meaningful. In other words, these conditions for learning apply to everyone, educators as well as students. As a starting point I will cite a few examples from articles in recent issues of *Educational Leadership* that I think exemplify the conditions.

I have grouped the examples by their relationship to particular conditions, but that is only for illustrative purposes. Most could have been used to illustrate other conditions because the conditions are not independent of one another. Alexander and Murphy (1998), who have documented the research base for the APA principles, caution that in "real-world learning situations" the principles are not separable entities but "remain inextricably intertwined." The conditions apply to any particular learning situation *as a whole*. Even so, I was pleased to find that the examples match surprisingly well with

the various conditions. For example, consider the first condition, which deals with the need for learning to be personally meaningful.

# 1. People learn well when what they learn is personally meaningful.

Jay Briar was a student at Thomas Jefferson High School
(McFaden and Nelson 1995) when he participated in a
research project at the Mason Neck National Wildlife
Refuge in northern Virginia. About the project he wrote:

> I'm flipping through the cable stations and as usual with 120
> channels to choose from, there is nothing worth watching. So I
> find myself watching C-SPAN. . . . Congressman Jim Moran was
> talking, and all of a sudden he is talking about deer hunts at
> Mason Neck [National Wildlife Refuge]. . . . He mentioned that
> managers there had given him data saying that the forest had
> been depleted seven-fold because of the deer overpopulation,
> and in doing so he referred to data collection done by students
> with the use of a deer enclosure. . . .

> It occurred to me that this was the first time in 10 years of
> school that something I had done was used for more than the
> purpose of grading, but for something that actually made a dif-
> ference. I want to thank you for the opportunity. It has given me
> more incentive to work than anything else that I have ever done
> in school. (p. 11)

Another example of how education can be personally meaningful comes from Paul Herdman (1994), who was reflecting on
why Outward Bound had such a powerful effect on his New
York City students. Herdman noted that the program is
described as *experience-based*, or *experiential*, education.

> To some, these terms mean simply learning by doing, but at
> George Washington [high school] we used physical experiences

not only to bring students' academic class work to life, but also as a bridge to a greater understanding of their own lives. For instance, we used rock climbing to teach young people about how to deal with the metaphorical walls that we all face in our lives. The primary purpose of asking a student to climb a 40-foot rock face is not to teach about the elements of climbing, but rather to show how to challenge self-perceived limitations, how to trust another human being, and how to break down into small manageable steps the apparently impossible walls one often faces. (p. 17)

Asked about his experience on "the wall," one of Herdman's students wrote:

Before we went rock climbing I had been so confident of myself. I was looking forward to start climbing. When we were ready to go up I said, "I want to be first." I started my climb and at the same time said to myself, "This is the easiest thing I have ever seen."

I was having fun until I got stuck. It was a place where there were no holds. It was all flat like the floor. I told myself, "It is impossible to go up." I looked down on Paul to see if he could give me direction. But he himself did not know how I could go on. I looked up and was near the top. I looked down once again to Paul and yelled at him that I was going to bail out. He said, "No, you can do it. I want you to think real hard." I was getting real angry at him and upset with myself.

Then I thought to myself it would be better if I could calm down as Paul said and follow instructions. That is where the poem that we read in the classroom went into my mind. I remember that there was this person in the poem that could not move because of a wall which represented a problem, but at the end he climbed the wall. I thought of all the problems that I had in my life and how I have to climb my way out of the walls. So, I could

not let this wall beat me, this small wall could not be the first
wall to conquer me, I was not going to let this wall take the best
of me. So I started up real fast, real smooth, just as I said I
would in the classroom. (pp. 18–19)

These examples suggest that experiences in the community
outside of school are likely to be more meaningful than anything teachers can provide in school. But classroom experiences can be meaningful, too. As an example of accelerated
schooling, Beth Keller (1995) described a 6th grade classroom
in an urban school where

> . . . students are learning about video development. The five-
> month unit, called Video Language, will culminate in a final
> video that the class will research, write, and produce. To
> gain an initial understanding, students have watched a num-
> ber of videos (including the ones students made the pre-
> vious year), then discussed their effectiveness. From this
> growing knowledge base, small teams have made short prac-
> tice videos, which they are now showing to the class for
> feedback.
>
> The youngsters intently watch a video of one of their peers
> demonstrating the use of hand tools. Pencils scribble furi-
> ously as students complete rating charts listing 15 essential
> elements of video production—eye contact, projection, ver-
> bal flow, costumes, props, entertainment value, instructional
> levels, and so on. The range of topics students have pro-
> posed for their videos reveals their wide interests—"Celebrat-
> ing the Iranian New Year," "Becoming an Orthodontist," "How
> to Find a Missing Person."
>
> "This project is 100 percent generated by the kids," says
> teacher Rich Carlson. "The students even came up with the
> criteria for which their videotapes should be graded." (p. 11)

A project planned by a group of teachers at the Bluebonnet
Applied Learning Academy in Fort Worth, Texas, is a good ex-
ample of students having a meaningful need to learn (Miller,
Shambaugh, Robinson, and Wimberly 1995). When the teach-
ers established a working partnership with the Fort Worth
Botanic Garden, their middle school

> . . . students now had a real reason to use multiple resources to
> master botanical research. They read texts from school and
> public libraries as well as those provided by the botanic staff;
> conducted online computer queries with fellow botany stu-
> dents; and explored government resources, including the local
> county extension agent. They collected data and applied math
> principles as they analyzed growth patterns and made infer-
> ences about growth conditions.
>
> The final results of the project began to multiply. Students' writ-
> ing skills soared as they developed, revised, edited, and field-
> tested accurate and descriptive brochures and trail guide
> maps. Students gained confidence in communications skills by
> interviewing experts, leading group tours, and fielding visitors'
> questions. (p. 23)

The idea that people learn best what they feel a need to learn
applies to adults as well as to children. When Tomm Elliott
(1993) confidently chose to return to the classroom after 10
years as a superintendent, he found teaching to be more difficult than he remembered.

> I began walking the dangerous line of pretending that I knew
> what I was doing while frantically trying to find out how to do
> it. I talked with my team leader, who gave me some ideas on
> how she planned her year. When I asked *what* we were sup-
> posed to teach she said, "Oh, there are district guidelines in

your cupboard, but we don't really use them." I talked with the
school's curriculum specialist, who told me: "Teach what
comes from the kids. Concentrate on the richness and texture
of the curriculum. Scope and sequence will follow." (p. 30)

Elliott didn't know how to use such advice.

I spent hours planning, but I couldn't make the plan book work.
My timing was off. I'd finish one activity too early, while
another one would take hours. I worked overtime checking
papers. (p. 30)

He was discouraged—but determined. He needed to learn,
and he did.

One day it hit me that the problem was that it was *my* curriculum and *my* planning that the kids weren't buying into. Sud-
denly the terms "richness and texture of the curriculum" took
on a whole new meaning. Little by little, things started to work.
The "richness and texture" began to come through. I began to
sense scope and sequence; I began to sense success. (p. 30)

## 2. People learn well when what they learn is challenging and they accept the challenge.

Challenge is tricky. We hear a lot these days about high standards, but as any teacher or learner knows, standards must be achievable or the learner will be frustrated and angry. And challenging learning tasks are effective only if the learner *accepts* the challenge. We have all seen students who, for one reason or another, refuse to try. For the person who wants the learner to learn, matching the challenge to the learner is the true challenge.

Christopher Cuozzo (1996–97) and a fellow teacher in Virginia Beach, Virginia, chose challenging goals for their 7th grade Advanced Life Science students by analyzing what real scientists do. For one class, they planned a nine-week unit on butterflies.

> We drew up a list of how scientists—and butterfly experts in particular—go about their work.
>
> - They keep a detailed, structured, field notebook.
>
> - They make careful, informed, and detailed observations.
>
> - They do research and keep abreast of current findings in the field.
>
> - They use, evaluate, and create field guides for identification.
>
> - They create butterfly gardens and rearing cages to use as observation stations.
>
> - They write articles for professional journals.

- They give presentations on their findings to the public and other professionals in the field.

Here was the list of activities that our students would engage in. (pp. 34–35)

Students who are presented with such a challenge—and accept it—find learning to be an exciting and satisfying experience. A student in Dubuque, Iowa, whose 5th grade class created a field guide to a local pond wrote in his journal:

> I felt like a real scientist. When I looked into the microscope and found the specimen, it was awesome. When you are done with the expedition, you go home and tell your mom and dad what you learned, and they practically don't even know what you are talking about. Six weeks ago I would never have known about pond life (Rugen and Hartl 1994, p. 20).

The idea that people learn when they set challenging but achievable goals is incorporated in good current professional development programs. Tom McGreal, an expert on teacher evaluation (Brandt 1996), told me:

> Beyond the intensive work with beginning teachers we've been talking about, most districts are creating what might be called a professional growth track for all tenured, experienced teach-ers—and this is where we're seeing some of the biggest changes. These programs are usually built around some ver-sion of individual goal setting, based on the recognition that it's absolutely essential for people to set their own goals. But what we used to call individual goals are now often referred to as pro-fessional development plans—long-term projects that teachers develop and carry out. (p. 31)

## 3. People learn well when what they learn is appropriate for their developmental level.

The notion of development can be interpreted in different ways. The example I will cite refers to educators' recognition of children's stages of cognitive development. Thomas Woehrle (1993) wrote about how staff members at Friends Academy in Locust Valley, New York, keep the developmental level of their students in mind as they plan service learning activities.

> In grades 1 and 2, we see the emergence of Stage 1. Children are becoming aware of their own feelings, but are not yet able to feel genuinely for others. Much effort must be invested in helping them learn that being a good neighbor means treating others as friends. Therefore, community service projects should go beyond making holiday decorations to delivering them in person to the residents of a nursing home. . . .

> While signs of Stage 2 development are seen in 8th and 9th grades, complete emergence takes place for the majority of our students in 10th grade during an overnight trip to New York City. This trip climaxes a required one-term course entitled "Poverty, Homelessness, and Community Service." The experience begins with students preparing an evening meal and sharing it with the occupants of several homeless shelters. Later that evening, they deliver sandwiches to homeless people who have taken up shelter in Grand Central Station. The following day, students prepare and serve lunch at various soup kitchens. How do our 10th graders react to this experience? They are amazed at the intelligence, insight, and experience of the homeless and hungry people they meet. These individuals are

no longer distant objects in need of help but people who have feelings, ideas, and interests "just like me." (pp. 40–41)

Of course, children differ not only in their cognitive development but in many other ways. Our next condition refers to these many differences and to people's need for personal autonomy.

## 4. People learn well when they can learn in their own way and have some degree of choice and control.

We have considerable evidence that students learn better when they use their preferred styles and special abilities. Howard Gardner's theory of multiple intelligences is one way of thinking about student differences that has attracted the attention of many educators in recent years. Thomas Hatch (1997) offers this advice based on research at Harvard's Project Zero, where he worked with Gardner.

> Instead of organizing the curriculum around the intelligences, organize around the child. We do not have to teach every child every subject in seven or eight different ways or ensure that every child develops every intelligence. Although we should expose children to a range of activities, every child does not, for example, need to develop musical intelligence or have mathematical or scientific concepts presented in musical form.
>
> Further, a knowledge of each child's intelligences and the ways in which he or she demonstrates them are merely tools that can help us understand and respond to that child's needs. If a child like Mark struggles in math or English, a teacher could draw on his sensitivity to people to help him in those subjects. The teacher might give him opportunities to survey his classmates and tabulate the results, or to cowrite biographies of family and friends. If, on the other hand, Kenny struggles in English or social studies, he may benefit more from writing assignments or debates that enable him to build on his skill as a negotiator. (p. 28)

Judith Zorfass and Harriet Copel (1995) demonstrated how individual choice affects learning in their explanation of an inquiry project for middle school students known as I-Search.

Teachers prompt students to reflect on what they are doing
and learning by asking: "What information are you finding inter-
esting?" and "What more do you want to learn?" . . . The goal is
for students to generate I-Search questions that they feel pas-
sionate about. Students recognize how important this is. When
we asked them what advice they would give novices embarking
on an I-Search process, one boy replied, "You better find a question you really care about because you will be working with
that question for six weeks." (p. 49)

Providing for participation when dealing with large numbers
of students under less than ideal conditions is difficult, but
encouraging students to assume responsibility for their own
learning can be productive. English teacher Katy Smith (1993)
told what happened when she and another teacher decided to
involve students in planning their own curriculum.

The biggest obstacle was the students' disbelief that we really
were going to live by the policy. Five days into the year, a student stopped by my desk and asked, "Are you guys really going
to use these policies, or did we do this just as an exercise to
see what it's like to make up rules?" I don't know whether I was
more surprised that he felt the need to ask, or whether he was
more surprised that my answer was "Yes!" . . .

The final result? On each of the local and departmental exams,
our classes' averages were virtually identical to those of tradi-
tionally taught classes for both the first and second semesters.
As of this writing, the state results are not yet in.

Why shift roles if test results are not going to change? Why is
negotiating curriculum better than dictating it? For one thing,
traditional tests do not yet assess the kinds of thinking and
problem-solving skills that our students developed throughout
this year. They became questioners, who know how to go after

the answers they seek. They also read and wrote extensively, with less moaning and groaning than we heard in the past— after all, it was their own questions they were reading and writing about. (pp. 36, 37)

## 5. People learn well when they use what they already know as they construct new knowledge.

The idea of "constructivism" is now generally well accepted by educators, although most of us are probably a little hazy about exactly what it means and how "constructive" teaching is different from other teaching. I have also included in this condition another idea basic to cognitive psychology, sometimes referred to as students' "prior knowledge." Despite their apparent familiarity, constructivism and prior knowledge are sophisticated concepts, so this brief discussion must necessarily be simplistic. I will just note that *the learner* must do the constructing, based on *the learner's* prior knowledge. All the educator can do is set things up to encourage that to happen.

Heckman, Confer, and Hakim (1994), whose story about pumpkins I used to illustrate feedback, told another story showing that sometimes teachers underestimate students' prior knowledge. They said two lst grade teachers were surprised when they

> . . . realized that the children had a significant base of knowledge . . . [that] exceeded even their teachers' most optimistic predictions. The children were sure that seeds needed water, sun, and soil in order to grow—but only in certain amounts: too much or too little would stop a seed from growing. The children explained that some soil was especially rich and fertile, and they told the teachers where in the neighborhood this kind of soil could be found.

At one point during the discussion, Manuel, usually quiet and withdrawn, began to talk about all the things he knew about seeds. Manuel, it seemed, had planted grass seeds next to a tree at home and had watched them grow. He had opened up seeds and found that they have minute baby leaves within. All seeds have tiny holes, Manuel explained, and the baby leaves emerge through the holes and grow into larger wing-like leaves. The teachers looked at each other with surprise as Manuel talked faster. He had smelled many different kinds of leaves, and he believed that each seed smells like the plant it will become. He further explained that there were different categories of seeds—flower seeds, food seeds, and plant seeds.

Later, Hakim and Confer examined the 1st grade science textbook to see what it would have presented to these children. The science book said three things: (1) plants need air, water, soil, and sun; (2) plants are green; and (3) plants are everywhere. Period. At best, turning to the science textbook would have seriously underestimated the knowledge that the children brought with them to school. At worst, it would have taught the children that their ideas were not valued, that true knowledge lay beyond them. Instead, a usually shy child had blossomed into a confident expert, and his 1st grade classmates had revealed an astounding amount of collective knowledge. (pp. 38–39)

Like other conditions for good learning, the idea that learners construct knowledge through personal experience applies to adults as well as children. In the Best Practice Project, Harvey Daniels (1996) and his colleagues have used direct experience to enlist the support of urban Chicago parents for progressive curriculum reforms.

We begin by handing out large index cards and invite everyone to think back over their development as a reader and writer (or their growth in math, science, the arts, or other subjects). We

then ask the group to take about 10 minutes to jot down
words, phrases, or doodles as particular moments or events
come to mind.

We then regather the group and ask a few people to share their
recollections—or, with permission, their partner's—with everyone. What unfolds are two kinds of stories: accounts of positive
literacy experiences, where the person was well-supported and
moved ahead; and tales of very destructive experiences, which
discouraged the person from reading and writing, sometimes
for good. Strikingly and sadly, the hurtful experiences usually
occurred in school; and the positive experiences, elsewhere.

Once parents reflect on their own experience as students, they
don't want to reminisce about their good old days. They don't
want their children to endure the same deadening seat work,
passive memorization, lockstep assignments, demoralizing
grading practices, and hurtful discipline. (p. 40)

Instead, Daniels testifies, parents endorse current approaches
to reading and writing when they themselves have used them.

## 6. People learn well when they have opportunities for social interaction.

When educators think about the social nature of learning, the first thing that comes to mind may be cooperative learning, which typically involves students working in pairs or small groups. Done well, cooperative learning can indeed help students learn, but the concept of learning as social activity is far broader. In fact, most of what we know has come through interaction with others, either in person or in other ways, such as through books and other media.

In schools, students are in a social setting not only when working in small groups but as part of regular class groupings. For several years Magdalene Lampert taught mathematics daily to a class of 5th graders while at the same time teaching her university classes. When I asked her (Brandt 1994a) what she did to cultivate a "community of inquiry," she said:

> All right, here's an example. We were working on rate and ratio in my class, so I gave my students this problem: if a car is going at a constant speed of 50 miles per hour, how far will it go in 10 minutes? Now, if you're familiar with elementary school students, you know that often they'll look at a problem and ask, "What should I do with the numbers?"
>
> Well, in this problem, there's a 50 and there's a 10. You could add them, subtract them, multiply, or divide them, right? Well, there's some sense that in time, speed, and distance problems, you're supposed to either multiply or divide. If you multiply, you get 500. That doesn't seem sensible, because if a car is going 50 miles an hour, in 10 minutes it's not going to go 500 miles.

So the first thing I would say is, "What do you think about this? How far do you think the car would go?" And let's just say that some students say 500 miles, and some say 5 miles. Then I would say, "Let's look at these two ideas. Let's look first at the 500 miles. Does that make sense? Have you ever been in a car that could go 500 miles in 10 minutes?" I wouldn't say, "That's wrong," or "That's ridiculous"; I'd say, "Let's think about it."

Now, that one is pretty straightforward, but let's look at 5 miles. When I gave this problem, that was the answer that most of my 5th graders originally asserted made sense. And if you think about riding in a car, it seems reasonable that you might go 5 miles in 10 minutes if you were going 50 miles an hour. But one of the students said, "I don't think that makes sense, because the car's supposed to be going 50 miles in an hour, and if it only goes 5 miles in 10 minutes, then in 20 minutes it'll go 10 miles, in 30 minutes it'll go 15 miles, and in an hour it'll only go 30 miles." So I asked, "What do the rest of you think about that?" and everyone went busily back to work, trying to figure out, "Well, gee, we thought it was 5. Ten into 50 is 5. Why doesn't that work?" The burden was on their shoulders to figure out why it didn't work.

Now, in this case, another student started making a diagram. She drew a line, and next to 10 minutes she put 5 miles, next to 20 minutes she put 10 miles, and so on. And using the diagram she figured out that we needed a number that, when multiplied by 6, would be close to 50. Eight was pretty close, but wasn't quite big enough, so eventually they decided that the car goes somewhere between 8 miles and 9 miles.

Now, it sounds like the kids are doing all the work. What's my job? Well, first of all, I asked questions that would lead them to question their assumptions. I monitored the discussion so that students could challenge one another in ways that were civil and relatively safe. And when their thinking came close to a big mathematical idea, I helped them to see those connections. (p. 29)

Learning is social in lots of ways. In recent years, students in some schools have participated in projects in which they exchange data over the Internet. One reason for the popularity of these programs is the opportunity they provide for interaction with other students and with experts. Monica Bradsher and Lucy Hagan (1995) noted that students and teachers who participate in the National Geographic Society's Kids Network are doing what scientists do.

> [T]hey participate in a scientific community devoted to learning about the world. Students pose and research questions about their local community, form hypotheses, collect data through experiments, and analyze results. The answers are largely unknown in advance, and the findings are of interest beyond the classroom. Students share their findings with their "colleagues" across the country, draw conclusions, discuss implications, and, finally, present their findings to their parents or the community. (p. 40)

A great deal of adult learning also takes place in a social context. Stephanie Pace Marshall and Connie Hatcher (1996) told of an incident in which teachers learned from one another at the Illinois Mathematics and Science Academy.

> After grading a homework assignment in which his students used Gauss's Law to solve an electric field problem, David Workman became convinced that some students could not visualize a field in three dimensions. Workman shared his observation with an astronomy teacher, who said that his own students had the same problem visualizing motion as seen from a moving Earth. (p. 42)

The two took the issue to other colleagues through a "Call for Dialogue," a structure for collaboration in the Academy. Workman explains:

We presented our observations to the 12 other faculty who responded to our "call." What seemed like a simple inquiry led to
a compelling insight: their students, too, had had this problem.

After a mathematics teacher described several exercises she
had found successful in helping her students visualize vector
fields, the two of us met with her to brainstorm visualization
activities. Later, we tried them with success in our classrooms.
Then, to share our findings with other colleagues, we wrote a
description of the exercises. (p. 42)

Powerful
LEARNING

36

## 7. People learn well when they get helpful feedback.

Feedback is a familiar concept to most of us. We say we are getting feedback when someone points out our errors or suggests ways to improve our performance. But we also can get feedback in more natural, less ego-bruising ways. Heckman, Confer, and Hakim (1994)

> . . . discovered that the children had a curious misconception: that pumpkins were filled with pumpkin juice. During the activity, a pumpkin fell and split open, exposing a rather dry interior. The children were shocked. Where was the juice? One child ventured that it had leaked out. Another thought that the worms drank it. This question, one that adults might never have thought of, dominated the entire discussion.
>
> The children cut open several pumpkins. Not one contained juice. Then, to further their study, the teachers took the class and several of the pumpkins to the home of one of the students, where the student's mother cut open more pumpkins to make *empanadas* (turnovers). Still no juice. As the mother cooked the pumpkin mixture, she intuitively addressed the issue. Pumpkin juice, she explained, is within its pulp. When the pulp is cooked, the juice is released, and she showed the children the hot juicy pumpkin mixture. (p. 38)

## 8. People learn well when they acquire and use strategies.

The teaching of strategies, sometimes called "learning how to learn," is somewhat controversial, because scholars disagree about whether or not schools should devote time trying to teach particular strategies explicitly. Some believe that, with good teaching, strategic behavior develops naturally as a byproduct of content learning. Others, though, say thinking skills can and should be taught directly. Both sides agree that learners need to acquire a repertoire of strategies and be able to use them effectively.

Steven Wolk (1994) explained why students in his classroom did well using the project approach.

> Before students begin their projects, they must write a plan and have me approve it. These project plans are an integral part of our classroom. They communicate the importance of thinking through the project in its entirety before actually beginning work. The plans must include topic questions that the students want to answer, possible resources, how they will show what they've learned, when their research will begin and end, and when they will present their finished project to the class. After completing their projects, students must also write a self-evaluation to help them become metacognitively aware of their learning. (pp. 42–43)

Based on extensive classroom observations, Russell Gersten (1996) described how Tapia, a highly effective bilingual teacher, helps her students learn to use thinking strategies needed for success in school.

[She] tells students they can use three sources of data to explain why they think a character is anxious. She lists the sources on a chart: actions, speech (or dialogue), and appearance. The class uses this list for discussing subsequent stories as well, and as a guide while writing in their journals. Tapia consistently challenges students to incorporate more complex structures in their analyses by referring to the list. For example, in response to student essays, she says, "None of you provided dialogue." Students then search for dialogue to support their inferences about a particular character.

Throughout our three years of observations, "You have to prove to me" was Tapia's consistent message. Teacher and peers evaluated, but never directly criticized, all attempts to develop or support an inference. Tapia continually prompted students to provide evidence for predictions, hypotheses, and inferences. (p. 19)

Some of the strategies that students need to learn involve relationships with other students. Leslie Farlow (1996) described the way a high school teacher taught her students how to get along with Adam, a junior with autism. At the time, Adam was

earning average grades in his classes. His parents hope[d] he [would] graduate with a regular diploma [the] next year."

Adam sometimes ha[d] trouble making friends, however. He frequently trie[d] to join in conversations by asking, "Do you know Barbara Bush?" and then repeating the question several times. Adam's autism also affect[ed] his ability to write essays and to answer inference questions.

His peers had primary responsibility for teaching Adam to engage appropriately in conversations, although they required some instruction to do so. His special education teacher taught all of the students in Adam's classes, and a large part of the general school body, about inclusion and friendships. Then she talked about how Adam needed to learn to make friends. She taught them how to redirect Adam to join their conversations with the same topic and gave them permission to tell Adam when they didn't like what he said or did.

Previously, students had ignored or avoided Adam when he tried to talk with them. Once they understood how to talk to him, however, his skills improved, and students included Adam in their groups more often. (p. 53)

Linda Lantieri, national director of Resolving Conflict Creatively, quotes 9th grader Branden telling how he learned to curb his aggressive behavior.

I just bullied people around. Got my own way. Didn't have many friends. Kids were scared of me. One day I punched this kid right in the face. Broke his glasses. At first I felt good about it. My friends thought I was cool. Then I saw he was crying. This kid hadn't done anything to me. I started feeling bad. When this program began at my school, my dad wanted me to join. I thought, "Yeah, right." This wasn't for me. But soon everything started to change. I began to get my respect another way. (Lantieri & Patti, 1996, p. 31)

## 9. People learn well when they experience a positive emotional climate.

Few would argue with the need for an orderly, supportive environment for learning. That is why schools using the James Comer Model begin with fundamental social skills even though their eventual goal is higher achievement scores. Christina Ramirez-Smith (1995) recalled how the Planning and Management Team at Magruder School in Newport News, Virginia, began its work.

> Team members agreed that their basic function was to create a positive school climate. Social behaviors such as saying "good morning" to everyone were only the beginning. Team members knew that they needed to actively model the behaviors that they expected from students, parents, and others in the school community. (p. 15)

The results of such efforts can be impressive. H. Jerome Freiberg (1996) quoted a high school English teacher whose school was using his Consistency Management and Cooperative Discipline program.

> It is early May. I look at my fifth-hour class and marvel at the climate of cooperation in a room full of 30 14-year-olds, hungry ones at that. They aren't disagreeing, sleeping, being insubordinate, or indifferent. They are enjoying learning and one another. Last year, I spent all my time trying to control my students. This year, the students know they matter. The negative attention-getting has stopped—there is no longer a need for it. They belong. (p. 32)

Students in Freiberg's program learn caring and cooperation behaviors. They apply for and are "hired" for jobs as "one-minute student managers." And they help decide what kind of classroom they should have.

> For example, in September, teachers and students establish rules for learning based on mutual needs by developing classroom constitutions or Magna Cartas. Here's a sample statement from Tina Smith's classroom: "We the students are entitled to: learn, feel safe, complain to the grievance committee [which the class created along with the constitution], ask questions, speak freely, have friends, not be put down, be treated fairly, share our feelings, get help, understand, and be treated kindly." All members of the classroom, including the teacher, sign the documents, which are in effect throughout the year. (p. 33)

Like the other conditions discussed in this book, a positive emotional climate is as important for adults as it is for children. I was reminded of that when I interviewed Al Mamary, former superintendent of the Johnson City, New York, school system, which had achieved amazingly high levels of student learning. When I asked him (Brandt 1994b) about outcome-based education, he talked about three principles.

> Here's the first one: all staff members will be involved in every major decision. The second idea is that we will always strive for 100 percent agreement, even if we have to go back many times. And third, we have an agreement that everybody will live by the agreements until we change them—and agreements should be changed now and then.

> Back in 1972, I said that a position in this district is not power. Instead, we said knowledge is power, *using* knowledge is power. We said—and we meant it—that we are co-workers and co-learners and co-doers. And I think that is why the district is where it is today. (pp. 24–25)

Mamary finally began talking about curriculum alignment and standards. I was relieved. "Now we're getting to the techniques of outcome-based education," I said. "Yes," he quickly replied, "but none of them makes a difference unless you have the right environment" (p. 25).

## 10. People learn well when the learning environment supports the intended learning.

The idea that the quality of learning is influenced by the total environment refers both to the social support the learner receives (discussed earlier) and to the "content" of the environment. We may learn the tune of a song played in the background even when we're working on something else and not paying conscious attention to the song. Our brains are constantly monitoring the total environment, receiving data through many channels—not just one. If what we hear is related to what we see and what we can also touch and examine, we will learn even more easily. For example, when we are putting together a piece of furniture or an unassembled toy, it is easier for most people to go back and forth between reading the directions and handling the pieces rather than reading the directions and then putting the item together.

Scott Thompson (1995) had this in mind when he argued that students should do service learning and have other school-related experiences outside school.

> Conventional classroom experiences are largely disconnected from the community and from real-world experience. Algebra and geometry, as taught to me in high school in the 1970s, were abstract, decontextualized, and not made relevant to my experience. I learned enough to kill the requirements and managed to avoid math altogether in postsecondary studies. Only in more recent years—in the course of project budgeting and other real-life problem solving—have I gained insight into why some people actually enjoy mathematics. Whether real-world

experiences are simulated in classrooms, as in microsociety schools, or actually take place in the community, workplace, wilderness, and other real-world settings, recontextualizing learning can be a powerful strategy. (p. 18)

Some current school curriculums are intended to achieve the "recontextualization" Thompson says is so necessary. In the Applications in Biology/Chemistry (ABC) program described by Prescott, Rinard, Cockerill, and Baker (1996), students learn scientific concepts by doing tasks that adults perform on the job, such as a bacteriologist using staining to identify microorganisms that cause food contamination. Designed for the middle 50 percent of the secondary student population, the program also uses

> . . . personal and societal contexts as well as workplace set-
> tings. Students may learn about nutritional requirements by
> exploring how these vary depending upon a person's dietary
> needs, age, and health. They may learn about pH in the context
> of a city's water-pollution controversy. Often teenagers are fea-
> tured in scenarios (for example, adolescents' dietary concerns,
> skin care, and sexual development are treated). Scenarios that
> address societal issues are often based on actual events, such
> as the Exxon Valdez oil spill, Calgene's development of a blue
> rose, and the Montreal Protocol (a 1987 agreement among
> nations calling for industrialized countries to reduce their use
> of chemicals that threaten the ozone layer). (p. 11)

Explaining the rationale for the ABC program, Prescott and others (1996) noted that, "For those students who do not think and learn in a predominantly abstract way, teaching science concepts in context provides a concrete and familiar framework for new ideas. This helps them comprehend and retain the information and gives them a rationale for doing so" (p. 11).

## Applying Knowledge About Learning

These excerpts demonstrate that examples of good teaching
can be used to illustrate principles of learning. But what about
the reverse? Can we consciously use knowledge about human
motivation and learning to improve schools? Educators associ-
ated with Rawsonville Elementary School in Ypsilanti, Michi-
gan, have shown it can be done. They made a deliberate effort
to put into practice what they called "achievement goal
theory." As reported by Rachel Buck Collopy and Theresa
Green (1995), the results were gratifying.

> Teachers have reported improved attendance, increased enthu-
> siasm for learning, and decreased discipline problems. As one
> teacher said, "I could never go back to teaching the way I did
> before." Referring to students' improved attitude toward learn-
> ing, a 20-year veteran wrote:

> Some students became so interested in some aspect of class-
> work that they did correlating activities on their own at home.
> Children brought in books, magazines, newspapers, and arti-
> facts that pertained to areas of study. They wrote plays, drew
> pictures, and made dioramas. . . . During our study of Japan,
> one little boy got so interested in haiku that he borrowed my
> books on it and began writing it—in school and at home. His
> mom reported that he was driving them "cuckoo" with his
> "haiku."

> Parents are very supportive of these efforts to change. Through
> formal and informal feedback, they report that their children
> have become more confident, more willing to take on chal-
> lenges, more excited about school, and better at working inde-
> pendently and with others. About her son, one parent wrote on
> a survey that she saw "great improvement in all areas—from a

student who was failing and had low self-esteem to an inter-ested, highly motivated *learner*!"

One clear example stands out of the extent to which the school community has embraced the changes brought about by achievement goal theory. At a recent PTO meeting, two parents suggested adding competitive rewards to an annual school event. Other parents told them that Rawsonville is not about winning and losing. It is about every child having access to the same enriching and educational experiences. It is about *learning*. (p. 40)

■   ■   ■

# Schools as Learning Organizations

# Schools as Learning Organizations

Leaders of schools, like leaders of businesses and hospitals, want their organizations to be flexible and responsive, able to change in accord with changing circumstances. The ideal organization is characterized as "self-renewing" or as a "learning organization," the term popularized by Peter Senge (1990) in *The Fifth Discipline*. The concept has at least two aspects. Not only are all the members, as individual persons, continually learning, but the organization itself is highly adaptable. Putting it that way raises the question of whether an organization can in fact be like a person in its ability to *learn*: to continually modify its shared knowledge and practices in accord with experience.

Earlier I listed the conditions that promote effective learning (Figure 2). Leaders who want staff members to continue learning should strive to create such conditions for the adult learners in their organizations. The conditions are derived from our view of effective learning by individuals, but also may apply to learning by the organization as a whole. Organizations, like human beings, are systems. Just as humans have a natural desire to know and understand, so do organizations seek to benefit themselves through exchange of information, both internally and with other systems. Just as some humans are better learners than others, some organizations are better than others at exchanging and making good use of information. But how far can we go in applying these principles to organizations?

In their quest to identify conditions fostering organizational learning in schools, Kenneth Leithwood and his coauthors (1997) have examined some of the theoretical literature on similarities between collective learning and individual learning—and found it wanting. Although "the metaphorical use of individual cognitive process to explain organizational learning has added considerably to our understanding," they say, such comparisons "cannot be adopted uncritically, even as metaphors" (p. 4). Partly for that reason, the authors avoid the term "learning organization" and talk instead about "organizational learning."

Although they reject the notion of "organizations as brains," Leithwood and his colleagues do accept the idea of collective "mind as activity rather than mind as entity. The collective mind, then, is to be found in patterns of behavior that range from 'intelligent' to 'stupid.' . . . From this perspective, mind can be 'knowledgeable' without containing knowledge" (p. 5).

With that loophole, then, and with the understanding that the analogy may be less than perfect, I invite you to ponder how research findings about the learning of individuals may also apply to organizations. Specifically, consider Figure 3 with its

**Figure 3**

## A COMPARISON OF LEARNING BY INDIVIDUALS AND ORGANIZATIONS

### Learning Individuals

Learn what is personally meaningful; what they feel a need to learn.

Learn when they accept challenging goals.

Go through developmental stages.

Learn in their own way.

Construct new knowledge by building on old.

Learn through social interaction.

Need feedback.

Develop and use strategies. (Learn how to learn.)

Learn well in a positive emotional climate.

Learn from the total environment, intended and unintended.

### Learning Organizations

Have an incentive structure that encourages adaptive behavior.

Have challenging but achievable shared goals.

Have members who can accurately identify the organization's stages of development.

Gather, process, and act upon information in ways best suited to their purposes.

Have an institutional knowledge base and processes for creating new ideas.

Exchange information frequently with relevant external sources.

Get feedback on products and services.

Continuously refine their basic processes.

Have a supportive organizational culture.

Are "open systems" sensitive to the external environment, including social, political, and economic conditions.

comparison of learning by individuals and learning by organizations such as schools or school systems.

**Strategies and feedback.** Just as individuals can improve their performance by acquiring thinking and reasoning strategies, so can organizations continuously improve their ability to gather information and use it to make decisions. To be a learning organization, schools need provisions for collection and analysis of data on matters that concern them, especially feedback from parents, employers, and other "customers."

**Knowledge construction.** Just as individuals construct their own knowledge in the messy process of learning, so do learning organizations draw upon their knowledge base to create ideas for new programs and services.

**Systems and subsystems.** Just as humans have subsystems (e.g., the circulatory system), so do organizations (e.g., the counseling service). In fact, the characteristics of a learning organization can probably be found not only in the organization as a whole but also in its parts, which are also systems as well as subsystems. Just as individuals learn through social interaction with others who think differently from themselves, learning organizations learn through the exchange of information among subsystems that, because they have dissimilar responsibilities, may function quite differently.

In summary, then, I have outlined two ways that schools can be learning organizations. They are by (1) creating conditions that support the learning of individual staff members, and

---

■ **Figure 4**

---

### CHARACTERISTICS OF SCHOOLS THAT ARE
### LEARNING ORGANIZATIONS

They have an incentive structure that encourages adaptive behavior.

They have challenging but achievable shared goals.

They have members who can accurately identify the organization's stages of development.

They gather, process, and act upon information in ways best suited to their purposes.

They have an institutional knowledge base and processes for creating new ideas.

They exchange information frequently with relevant external sources.

They get feedback on products and services.

They continuously refine their basic processes.

They have a supportive organizational culture.

They are "open systems" sensitive to the external environment, including social, political, and economic conditions.

---

(2) realigning the structure and processes of the entire organization to support continuous adaptation and change.

When discussing conditions that encourage learning by individuals, I mentioned that psychologists caution against treating principles of learning separately from one another. They

advise that the principles (conditions) should be seen as closely related aspects of a single situation. Individuals learn best when the content is meaningful to them *and* they have opportunities for social interaction *and* the environment supports the learning.

That idea applies to organizations as well. To check whether a school is functioning as a learning organization, its staff members and others need to consider the list of characteristics not as a checklist but as elements of the whole.

■　　■　　■

# Powerful Learning in the Learning Organization

# Powerful Learning in the Learning Organization

To show how schools and school systems can function as learning organizations, I will again cite some examples from *Educational Leadership*.

## 1. Learning organizations have an incentive structure that encourages adaptive behavior.

Just as individuals learn when they are motivated to learn, organizations learn when they have a reason. The incentives to learn may be material or psychological, but one form of incentive that everyone understands is money. Michael Murphy and Alice Miller (1996) described a program their district devised to improve staff members' technological skills.

> In Southlake, Texas, earlier this year, the following professional development activities took place. A group of new teachers attended an after-school workshop on Windows software. A school bus driver participated in an all-day "Super Saturday" workshop to find out what word processing is all about. And a veteran special education teacher used a computer graphics program to create a picture book—one of several computerized solutions she came up with to help some of her life skills students communicate with classmates.
>
> What do these people have in common? None was forced to attend inservices. None earned continuing education credits for his or her extra work. What they did earn, however, were cash stipends—$525 for the teachers and $300 for the bus driver. All work for the Carroll Independent School District, a small suburban district midway between Dallas and Ft. Worth. The district's performance-based technology competency program is designed to motivate all employees to learn new technological skills and to impart that knowledge to students. The program rewards professional growth, involves adult learners in their own planning, and correlates individual needs with school and district goals. (p. 54)

Incentives exist at all levels of an organization. Financial incentives may be individual, like those in Carroll, Texas, or organizational. Stephen Fink, assistant superintendent, wrote in 1992 that the Edmonds, Washington, school district had paid attention to incentives when it reorganized its categorical programs. "Our goal was an integrated special, compensatory, and basic education service delivery model that would provide effective instruction for all students. The district's only preconceived outcome was that all students would learn at a high level of mastery." (p. 42)

The Edmonds district was an organization engaged in "learning" new behaviors. To do so, it needed a set of incentives consistent with the new direction.

> A major hurdle to improving the achievement of low-performing and handicapped students was the various categorical program regulations. The notion of targeted funds in and of itself is not detrimental, but use of the funds is laden with regulations that curb creative thinking. From the federal to the state level, infrastructures supporting each categorical program have served to isolate and institutionalize these programs.
>
> The Edmonds School District has not received any special waivers for program regulations. To support schools in their creative deployment of categorical resources, the district "blends" federal, state, and local dollars according to each school's needs. Due to federal regulations that require extensive record keeping to track each employee's "time and effort," managing the "blending" process is highly labor-intensive. However, we believe it is necessary to promote school-centered decision making and reform. (Fink 1992, p. 42)

## 2. Learning organizations have challenging but achievable shared goals.

Most organizations have publicly stated goals. Learning organizations have especially demanding goals that actually guide the organization and somehow gain the dedication of staff and other constituents. Adele Corbett (1996), assistant superintendent, and her coauthors told how the Great Valley, Pennsylvania, School District developed widespread commitment to a locally initiated sexual harassment prevention program.

> Convincing a school board or an administrative team that denial is not the best route requires both investigation and education. As we began exploring the issue, it quickly became apparent that our staff, students, and parents were relatively naive about sexual harassment. . . . To awaken a cautious school board to the realities of sexual harassment in a high school environment, we used a video. . . . They came back believers. . . . Once the school board was sold and we received the grant, the next step was to make staff members aware. . . . We also had to familiarize everyone with district policies and procedures. . . . When the training was completed, teachers volunteered to get the process started in their schools and, eventually, to train students. . . .
>
> It is difficult to motivate community members to get involved in problems like sexual harassment. We began our outreach efforts when we began the inservice teacher training, using focus groups, parent-teacher organization forums, and parent education seminars. As in many busy suburban communities, however, these meetings were not heavily attended. So, to make sure the public was aware of our efforts, we turned to our school district's access TV channel. At regular intervals, we pro-

vided information about sexual harassment prevention and the
nature of our instruction at the elementary, middle, and high
school levels. . . . And we networked with other community
organizations, such as the American Association of University
Women. (pp. 69–70)

In any organization, some goals may legitimately be concerned with changing organizational processes, such as the
way the system uses information technology or communi-
cates with various audiences. In a school district, the most
important goals are those dealing with student learning. Kevin
Castner and his coauthors (1993) explained an ambitious plan
developed by the Frederick County, Maryland, schools
intended to ensure student achievement of five "Essential
Learner Behaviors."

> In each curricular area, essential learner behaviors are sup-
> ported by essential discipline goals, which, in turn, are supported
> by essential course objectives. For instance, a task that requires
> 7th graders to plan a field trip to a museum in Washington,
> D.C., could meet two essential course objectives: (1) collect,
> organize, represent, and interpret data and (2) make estimates
> appropriate to given situations.

These 7th grade objectives support our K–12 mathematics
discipline goal: to develop mathematical skills and reasoning
abilities needed for problem solving. In addition, the lesson
helps students gain skills in effective communication, social
cooperation, and citizenship. Each level and grade of schooling, beginning in kindergarten, uses the foundation of individual courses and disciplines to build toward mastery of the
learner behaviors at the top of the pyramid. (p. 46)

### 3. Learning organizations have members who can accurately identify the organization's stages of development.

Organizations, like people, change over time. We can compare the phases of growth (and decline) of organizations to the developmental stages children go through as they move from infancy to childhood to adolescence to adulthood. In learning organizations, people can articulate the changes they are consciously trying to make and can identify where they are in the process.

Ruth Wade (1997), principal of Poquonock School in Windsor, Connecticut, reported that student behavior at her school had markedly improved.

> [C]hildren enjoy racial harmony and a sense of community, responsibility, and empowerment. A survey we conducted recently showed that our students rarely experience race-related problems at school. And they display relatively few behavior problems. (p. 34)

Five years earlier, the situation had been very different.

> In September 1992, we greeted a number of hostile students and families who were not happy about being forced to attend our school. The result was a dramatic increase in behavior problems and racial incidents, problems that faculty members were unprepared to deal with.
>
> To improve schoolwide behavior and begin to build a new sense of community, our staff formed a Behavior Committee. We reluctantly set up a schoolwide Assertive Discipline Plan,

designed to extinguish inappropriate behavior. . . . Our assessment showed that our system was working in the short run; we
saw improved behavior and a new school spirit and camarade-
rie. But we saw, too, that many students weren't concerned
about the impact of their behavior on others or about perma-
nently displaying more responsible behavior; they were motivated solely by rewards. . . . Clearly we were manipulating and
controlling behavior instead of instilling sound values. (p. 34)

Wade's article suggests that members of a learning organization are aware that their institution does not arrive at its final
destination instantly but must develop one step at a time.
They have a clear sense of what they're trying to do, what
progress they have made, and what still needs to be done.
Wade recalled:

After some reading, reflection, and visits to schools with similar
problems, we decided to change our approach. . . . We dropped
Assertive Discipline, our detention room, and the monthly
award themes. Much to our surprise, students did not seem to
miss the awards, and their behavior got no worse. One might
conclude from these results that Assertive Discipline had con-
trolled misbehavior or that, with time, the initial furor over re-
districting had dissipated. Both conclusions are probably true
to some degree. Still, we had not generated a sense of owner-
ship and community among students and their families. . . .

Over the next two years, we initiated many changes. We replaced
rewards with schoolwide celebrations and replaced conse-
quences with problem solving. Now when students misbehave,
we encourage them to reflect on their behavior and its effect on
others. We then ask them to come up with a plan for restitution
(if appropriate) or other solution to the problem. . . . As we
have changed our focus from teacher solutions to student
solutions, and given students more responsibility, our school
climate has improved dramatically. (pp. 35, 36)

The Reed Union School District in Tiburon, California, under-
took a different kind of change. Robert Kessler (1992), superintendent, looked back on his district's multiyear effort to use
shared decision making in development of the annual budget.

> Getting started wasn't easy. Several years ago, as part of a coun-
> tywide professional development project, the Reed Board of
> Trustees made an initial commitment to developing teacher
> involvement in decision making. Once the Management Team
> was in place, we hired a trainer to help us analyze our personal
> styles and develop effective group dynamics. Out of the train-
> ing process came our Team Agreements: to commit to operate
> by consensus, respect one another's styles, speak honestly,
> and advocate the team's decisions to our constituencies.
> Taking the time to work out these agreements was critical
> for success. . . .
>
> Recently, the budget situation throughout California has created
> our greatest challenge yet. The lack of cost-of-living increases
> in state revenue to local districts means that budgeting for
> even minimal salary increases is increasingly difficult. District
> staff began to question whether teacher interests are best
> served through traditional, adversarial bargaining or through a
> more collaborative process. It is a mark of commitment to
> shared decision making that the district and the teachers' asso-
> ciation have agreed to broaden the scope of our Management
> Team to include all contract negotiations. (pp. 36–37, 38)

## 4. Learning organizations gather, process, and act upon information in ways best suited to their purposes.

Organizations, like people, are different from one another, so they probably need to "learn" differently too. To illustrate this idea, we need to look beyond the use of data—very important in itself— to see how learning organizations use processes "best suited to their purposes."

For example, Stephen Gross (1996) described how the Vermont State Department of Education went about establishing the Vermont Common Core of Learning, an effort to set direction for curriculum throughout the state. Recognizing that local school people might consider the initiative a dangerous intrusion and might therefore ignore the resulting document, the Department of Education decided to

> . . . bring as many people as possible into the process and use
> their ideas to create a powerful shared vision for the future. . . .
> Instead of leaving the work to a blue-ribbon panel, we would go
> to the people of our state with a blank slate and use the focus
> forum process to ask some powerful questions about the needs
> of learners for the 21st century. In this way, committee mem-
> bers would shift their roles from writers to researchers and
> investigators. By bringing so many people into the act of invent-
> ing, perhaps we would have stronger results. (pp. 50–51)

When local districts adopt innovative curriculums, they may have the opposite problem. New ideas will probably not be ig-nored, but they may provoke storms of protest. To avoid that, when the Ames, Iowa, Community School District began using

**66**

a new mathematics program, Margaret Meyer and her coauthors (1996) listened for, and carefully responded to, parents' concerns.

> At the beginning of the school year, the district sent parents letters describing the project and requesting permission to share student work as a part of the data collection. Every school involved held meetings with parents to give them information and to address their concerns. As the program began, school staff kept an informal record of parents' questions and concerns, including those expressed at meetings, in telephone calls, interviews, and written surveys.
>
> After a number of contacts with parents, the nature of their concerns became clear. . . . District officials began addressing these concerns by classifying them into five general categories, each of which called for a different type of response. The least serious concerns were those of parents wondering how to support the program. These were followed by concerns resulting from misinformation or no information, concerns about program implementation, and concerns about whether teachers or researchers could be trusted. Most serious were the concerns based on traditional beliefs about schooling.
>
> We should point out that by degree of seriousness we are referring to the nature of the response required by the school district. *All* parent concerns are serious to the parents who have them, and we need to recognize and respect this. For a school district, however, some misgivings have more serious consequences if they are ignored or addressed inappropriately. In other words, if the district does not handle it in a timely and appropriate manner, a category two concern can quickly escalate into a category three or four concern. (p. 55)

The Quality movement, inspired by the work of W. Edwards Deming and others, stresses the value of collecting and analyz-

ing data. Patricia Abernethy, superintendent, and Richard
Serfass, assistant superintendent (1992), described the use
of quality management tools in the Cherry Hill, New Jersey,
public schools.

> The first issue we decided to address was attendance at the dis-
> trict high school. To do so, we used a detailed problem-solving
> process called the Quality Improvement Story. . . . As our
> theme for improvement, we chose: *decrease high school tardi-
> ness and increase attendance.* . . . After we corrected [the] tardy
> data, the high school attendance rate was up to a monthly aver-
> age of 92 percent. Our next step was to determine the root
> causes of nonattendance for the remaining 8 percent of stu-
> dents' absences. . . . Next we formulated countermeasures/po-
> tential solutions to those root causes that were within our
> control to change. . . . The Total Quality tools helped us focus
> on the problem *one step at a time.* . . . we are convinced that the
> process presents valuable opportunities to systematically bring
> about change in our school system. (pp. 14, 15, 17)

## 5. Learning organizations have an institutional knowledge base and processes for creating new ideas.

The idea of an institutional knowledge base and related processes for creating new ideas is parallel to the notion that individuals construct new knowledge by building on prior knowledge. What kind of processes might an organization use to strengthen its knowledge base and encourage creative ideas?

A good example may be CADRE—Career Development Reinforcing Excellence—developed by the Illinois Mathematics and Science Academy to replace traditional practices in supervision, evaluation, and professional development (Marshall and Hatcher 1996). Faculty members progress through a series of interdependent contractual relationships with the Academy beginning with an initial two-year contract and leading to participation in the school's Collaborative Accountability Network. At each stage,

> the Academy expects teachers to model lifelong learning, to generate a change in how their students view and organize the world, and to actively promote the Academy as an exemplary educational laboratory. Second, the Academy expects teachers' professional dialogue to conform to a number of conditions based on mutual respect and trust. For example, teachers need to adopt a collaborative role rather than an advocacy role, be open to learning from one another, and be willing to embrace risk.
>
> In turn, the Academy makes a commitment to teachers to provide them a climate that fosters their accomplishment of these standards and conditions. For example, the Academy gives

them the necessary resources and support for their continued professional development, involves them in making decisions in which they are stakeholders in the outcomes, and provides them the academic freedom to explore controversial issues. . . .

Faculty report that they are sharing more ideas and resources across disciplines; interacting with their colleagues with greater honesty and humility; collaborating more to resolve problems; producing more materials and integrative courses and projects; and interacting more with the entire community. Many say that while CADRE does not actually create collaboration, it provides support for it through a formal structure. (pp. 44, 45)

Other schools use different ways to inspire teachers to use their shared knowledge base creatively. Richard Ackerman and his coauthors (1966) note that professional development programs "are increasingly moving away from presentations by experts and toward programs that involve administrators and teachers as facilitators of their own renewal and growth." Use of case studies is a method they have found particularly productive.

The premise underlying our work is that the story form is a sense-making tool for educators. Writing their own stories can help them to better understand and share their theories of practice and dilemmas, and explore new possibilities with one another. At some point, participants begin to think differently— more critically and less self-centeredly. They are challenged and inspired to think more deeply about their practice and investigate ways to solve problems . . . to make sense out of past behaviors and actions and generate new ideas. (pp. 21, 23)

## 6. Learning organizations exchange information frequently with relevant external sources.

Just as individuals learn by interacting with other people, organizations also learn from one another. R. Clarke Fowler and Kathy Klebs Corley (1996) described how Saltonstall Elementary School in Salem, Massachusetts, connects with parents and community agencies.

> As experienced educators, we know that there are parents in every class who, without being asked, will find ways to become involved with their child's school. Other families are extremely difficult to reach, no matter what we do. To connect with these parents, we've established a Parent Center in a room originally used as a classroom.

> Our Parent Center, a 900-square-foot room on the first floor, is an inviting space with a couch, comfortable chairs, sewing machines, local newspapers (*The Salem Evening News* and *El Pointa*), toys for young children, and a pot of coffee warming on the stove. On hand is a full-time paid parent coordinator, who is available to meet with parents and refer them to the appropriate services. Currently, we are fortunate to have in this position a woman who is a long-term resident of the city who speaks both Spanish and English.

> We have contracted with two local agencies, North Shore Children's Hospital and KIDNET, to provide services to students and families in need. These contracts allow the school and the respective social service agency to share information. Because the Parent Center is linked with the school's networked computer system, we can also share appropriate information with teachers who are involved with the students. (p. 25)

The difference between settings in which information is freely
exchanged and those where it is not is made dramatically
clear in Tony Wagner's (1997) account of a New Hampshire
regional school district where "five quiet, picturesque villages
. . . [had] been at war with one another" (p. 28). The climate
began to change as the result of a series of meetings led by
Wagner in which board and community members, parents,
teachers, and high school students discussed their goals,
values, and immediate priorities.

In February, the board and the union agreed on a new teacher
contract in record time, and it contained the first raise for
teachers in nearly five years. But many people were concerned
about what would happen when the school budget came up for
approval at the March town meeting. No one could have
guessed the outcome: A substantially increased budget passed
with a voice vote and no vocal dissension—for the first time in
several years.

At the last of the four town meetings, we asked for volunteers
to consider next steps. More than 60 people indicated an inter-
est in working on one of three committees: one to create a mission statement for the district that would spell out what all
White Mountain graduates should know and be able to do; one
to create a statement of core values; and one to look at immediate school improvement priorities. Each committee began to
work on a report and recommendations for next steps.

Then an unexpected test of our newfound spirit of cooperation
occurred: In the fall of 1996, a coach was suspended for unpro-
fessional behavior. The disciplinary actions taken by the principal and by the superintendent were extremely controversial,
and so the board decided to review the case. The turnout for
the meeting was enormous. Both the board and the community

were split down the middle by the issue, and many privately feared that this controversy would destroy the civility the community had struggled to achieve. But this time there was no name-calling, no shouting. The townspeople seemed to have learned to discuss their disagreements in a different spirit. (p. 28)

# 7. Learning organizations get feedback on products and services.

An important benefit from interacting with others is feedback. Educators are sometimes wary of feedback, because they seem to get it from all directions. Nevertheless, feedback is valuable. And some schools do a better job of listening for and acting upon the feedback available to them, even from the most obvious sources. Mary Koski (1993), a teacher at Thompson Junior High in St. Charles, Illinois, recalled the staff-initiated changes her school district had made in recent years.

> We have now entered another step of the process, embedding the changes, working to meet the needs of our "customers," the students. At the end of each nine-week period, we ask the students to evaluate the work just done. Based on their input, we revise the curriculum. Student committees advise the principal on proposed changes at school, and students serve on the Total Quality teams, working to improve the transportation system, the cafeteria, and the high school's integrated American Studies class. As members of the strategic planning committee, they help define the district's future goals in curriculum, instruction, communication, finances, facilities, and technology.

> The students remind us on a daily basis to continue the changes we have begun. Only three days after the outcome-based science fair discussion, I moved the chairs in my classroom back into rows. We hadn't touched the textbook in months, and I felt a need to cover a topic. Because we had always learned about earth history and fossils in February, we began reading the textbook, making plaster fossils, and creating the traditional 4.5 billion year timeline with glued-on trilobites, dinosaurs, birds, and mammals.

Finally Ben asked, "Mrs. Koski, why are we just using the books? Why aren't we looking for real fossils and calling up scientists to see what they know about dinosaurs?" I knew then that, like the dinosaurs on the timeline, I could not bring the old ways back to life, nor would I choose to. I was glad my students would keep reminding me of that even when I forgot. (p. 52)

To get the feedback they need, schools must demonstrate a high degree of openness and trust. B.J. Meadows, principal, and her coauthors (1993) told about a highly unusual project in which parents were invited to observe classes, in some cases using video recorders,

> . . . to determine whether behaviors observed in classrooms supported our stated beliefs about building self-esteem. For example, when a teacher coaches students to make their writing personal by using their own thinking, she is supporting the belief that experiences that allow for individual differences contribute to self-esteem.

> As a result of the FOCUS project, we now have a better idea of how well classroom practices are fostering the school's 17 beliefs about improving students' self-esteem. . . . We have seen several positive results. . . . First, some teachers are planning to examine their teaching and evaluation methods using these findings as a guide to improve students' performance. . . . Second, the process has brought parents and staff members closer together. . . . Third, we now know what student behaviors indicating self-esteem occur most and least frequently. For example, parents rarely observed students learning from their mistakes. . . . The parent observations are giving us a clearer picture of what we need to continue doing well and what we need to improve. (pp. 33, 34)

## 8. Learning organizations continuously refine their basic processes.

A closely related characteristic of schools as learning organizations is their attention to processes, some of which have to do with communicating with constituents, gathering and using data, getting feedback, and the other characteristics already discussed. According to assistant superintendent Jan Vondra (1996), the Snowline, California, Unified School District has made significant changes in the way it relates to conservative parents. Describing how parents and teachers in one school resolved a conflict over instructional materials and how the school system helped another group of parents establish a traditionalist alternative school, Vondra offered advice to educators who may be involved in similar controversies in their own communities.

We are still learning about public schools and conflict, but we have found that certain strategies are particularly useful in finding common ground. Here are five of them. We hope other educators, parents, and community members can profit from our experience.

1. Establish policies that (a) the school district's board of trustees clearly support and (b) define the role of parents and the community in public schools, the role of teaching about religion in schools, and the role of civic debate about controversial issues. . . .

2. Encourage the participation of every segment of the community, so that everyone takes responsibility for the education of our children. . . .

3. Recognize parents as having the primary responsibility for the upbringing of their children, including the children's education. . . .

4. Avoid labels or educational jargon—two of the major obstacles to finding common ground. . . .

5. Be aware that in attempting to find common ground, your own unrecognized prejudices may often surface. We began five years ago with the naive assumption that we would create an open, accepting environment and would help others recognize their narrow perspectives. Compromise and an effort to reflect the community's values and beliefs come easy when we agree with the community and the compromise! What is more difficult is to actually compromise and publicly support a different philosophy because we believe in the rights and responsibilities of parents in bringing up their own children. (pp. 78–79)

The "basic processes" schools develop and refine are similar to the "learning to learn" strategies used by individuals. The connection between the two was made explicit by Robert Calfee and Clay Wadleigh (1992), who reported that a program used in more than 100 schools across the United States had evolved from a classroom-based reading program to a school-based Inquiring School model. "These schools had become 'communities of inquiry,' not by external mandate, not by top-down dictate, not through research. Instead, they had transferred structures and strategies for effective language use from the classroom to the school." (p. 28)

Inquiry, Calfee and Wadleigh pointed out, requires "a paradigm shift. . . . Schools are known for their chaotic agendas, shortage of time, isolation of people, and top-down management. Inquiry, on the other hand, requires a clear focus, a slow pace for reflection, social interactions, and genuine collaboration" (1992, p. 28).

To help readers envision what an inquiring school is like, the authors offered "a few concrete sketches," including one of North Shoreview Elementary, a school serving a multicultural, blue-collar neighborhood in San Mateo, California.

> At North Shoreview, Principal Evelyn Taylor was the initial cata-lyst for change. Quickly handing over the reins to teacher com-mittees, she sparked this dialogue:
>
> - "What do you need to make the READ ideas work?"
>
> - "Smaller classes."
>
> - "How can we make that happen? What can we do with what we have?"
>
> The dialogue was genuine. The faculty wrestled with cost-bene-fit questions. They proposed and implemented a schoolwide plan for integrating regular and categorical programs to achieve more workable student-teacher ratios (still large by national standards, to be sure). . . . They took on the respon-sibility for leadership not from a bureaucratic mandate, but through a problem-solving process directly supported by READ strategies. (pp. 28, 30)

While some processes develop gradually, as apparently hap-pened in the Project READ schools, they may also come about in response to urgent need. That was what L.E. Scarr (1992), superintendent, had in mind when he thoroughly reorganized the 38,000-student Lake Washington school district in Kirk-

land, Washington. The 2,200 staff members, including central office staff, building administrators, and support personnel, were grouped into four work teams, three of them regional teams organized around the three high schools. The fourth team was responsible for providing

> . . . services to schools and teams including business, facilities, and personnel. No longer do we have a Director of Elementary or Secondary Education or a Technology Supervisor and Curriculum Director. These specialized and differentiated functions have been redesigned by each team to meet schools' needs.
>
> Each team is responsible for assisting schools in developing a three-year strategy to implement the district's restructuring vision in three major areas: use of time; [use of] staff members; and community, business, and parent partnerships. Each team is also charged with supporting the operational needs of schools and with developing plans to allocate resources. Since the teams are self-regulating, they have developed the structures that guide them including budget allocation, communication, organizational structure, and decision making.
>
> Bureaucracies break work down into a series of discrete tasks. Educating students is not a series of specialized jobs but a set of integrated steps and responsibilities. We have attempted to implement an organizational structure that supports this reality. (pp. 69–70)

# 9. Learning organizations have supportive organizational cultures.

The literature on school climate and school culture is very extensive. I will oversimplify by saying the culture should be *humane*—psychologically comfortable, with warm human relationships—and *professionally supportive*—a place where people have the tools and training they need, and where they have opportunities to collaborate and learn from others.

Pauline Sahakian and John Stockton, staff members of a high school in Clovis, California, illustrated both aspects of "supportive" with a teacher's description of what she saw when she arrived for a meeting at which teachers were to discuss their observations of one another's classes.

> As I stepped through the doorway of my administrator's office, I was greeted by a checkered tablecloth, baskets of muffins and fruit, and a thermos of coffee. A party? No. The ever-dreaded administrator's postobservation conference!

> Our administrator had set the stage for the English Department's first collaborative postobservation conference. The ambience created a friendly, relaxed forum for discussing the instructional methodologies and philosophies of six teacher triads.

> Along with our administrator, we had all observed one another teach. Now we gathered to reflect on our practices in an effort to grow both personally and as a department of professional educators. (Sahakian and Stockton 1996, p. 50)

The culture in some schools is not at all like the one just described. Researcher Milbrey McLaughlin (1992), Stanford

University, found major differences among school systems in their relationships with teachers and in the teachers' responses. To highlight the differences, she contrasted two California districts she called Oak Valley and Mostaza (not their real names).

> The teachers in the Oak Valley School District speak of themselves as respected professionals. Their comments underscore the trust and authority they feel the district places in them through various policies and practices. They emphasize that they are proud to be teachers in their district.
>
> The teachers in the Mostaza School District use fundamentally different language. They speak of being "infantalized" by district actions. They describe being "treated as automatons," not professionals. They voice concerns of not being trusted or respected, and a number of them say they would not recommend Mostaza as a place to teach. (p. 33)

McLaughlin and her fellow researchers were concerned not just with teachers' satisfaction but with the effects of the organizational climate on professional community and on school effectiveness.

> These different views of professional identity and worth influence much more than teachers' "happiness quotient"; they shape practice, morale, and commitment. The Oak Valley School District's vital sense of professionalism and trust translated into pride of practice, willingness to go the extra bit, and extraordinary commitment to district and job. (p. 34)

## 10. Learning organizations are "open systems" sensitive to the external environment, including social, political, and economic conditions.

The way the Gwinnett County, Georgia, public schools created a new set of standards for student writing is a good example of what it means to be an "open system." Kate Kirby-Lipton and her coauthors (1996) wrote:

> We knew it would be essential to involve parents in the standards-setting process. . . . We had just survived a year of intense scrutiny of our instructional program by our community, and parents welcomed involvement in any improvement effort. More than 125 parents volunteered. Of those, we selected a group of 50 geographically representative parents (rural, urban, and so on). They joined 30 teachers in setting the standards during a two-week workshop.
>
> Using both the state's rubrics for writing and the anchor papers, we trained parents and teachers to score papers holistically—that is, not trait by trait. We then selected a number of papers to represent levels 1–4 of the state's rubric for middle schools and high schools and the six stages for elementary schools. . . .
>
> To validate whether the anchor papers were on target, we submitted our high school papers to the University of Georgia for review. There, the director of the freshman writing program concluded that the students who had produced the most highly rated papers were on track for admission to that university and that writers of the lower-rated papers would need further academic assistance to be eligible for admission. (p. 31)

What makes the Gwinnett County story especially notable is that school officials not only involved parents in setting

standards for student achievement but also checked with the state university, an important "customer."

Another good example of a system attuned to its environment is the way the New Haven, Connecticut, public schools established a comprehensive social development project. Roger Weissberg and his coauthors (1997) wrote:

> In 1987, the superintendent convened a task force—including educators, parents, students, community leaders, university researchers, and human service providers—to assess the high-risk behaviors of students that lead to drug use, teen pregnancy, AIDS, delinquency, truancy, and school failure. Through in-depth surveys, the task force found that a significant proportion of New Haven's high school students engaged in behaviors that jeopardized their academic performance, health, and safety. . . .
>
> The New Haven task force noted that the same students experienced several problems simultaneously—problems that seemed to have common roots, such as poor problem-solving and communication skills; antisocial attitudes about fighting and education; limited constructive after-school opportunities; and a lack of guidance and monitoring by adults who are positive role models. The task force recommended that New Haven create a comprehensive K–12 social development curriculum to address these needs.
>
> The superintendent and board of education established a district-level Department of Social Development—with a supervisor and staff of facilitators—that coordinated all prevention and health promotion initiatives. . . . Curriculum committees at all grade levels developed a K–12 scope and sequence for the Social Development curriculum. . . . Throughout the process, the committees considered federal standards, state mandates,

and the priorities of local educators, parents, community members, and students; and they obtained the support of university psychologists. (pp. 37, 38)

## Engaging the Broader Community

To sum up, here are two more brief stories that show how schools and school districts can be good learners. Both reveal several of the characteristics of learning organizations, but they focus primarily on the way the organization relates to its external environment, including students, family members, the immediate community, and the broader society. First, a heartening tale of a single school, Pio Pico Elementary School in Santa Ana, California.

Martie Lubetkin (1996), speech/language specialist, wrote that the process began when a group of parents, worried about the safety of their children because of gangs and drug sales in the neighborhood, developed a plan to escort their children to and from school. The informal parents group became the Safety Committee that, with the school principal as facilitator, expanded into a Neighborhood Association. Enlisting the help of the local police department, they got the drug problem under control and decided to hold Operacio'n Limpieza (Operation Clean-Up), which has become an annual event.

> The area has remained clean and well cared for, and the people living there take the responsibility to keep it so. And that's not all. In the last four years, crime in the community has dropped by approximately 35 percent. . . . The clean-up was just the first step in reaching out to the families and the community, and in enlisting the help of local businesses. The school's extended family has grown, and the community has become more involved in the school. . . . The parents have become advocates for their children's education. They are interested and involved

in what happens at school, and they are determined to help
their children achieve.

The Pio Pico vision of "lifelong learners, eager and well prepared to make positive contributions to a diverse global society" will take years to evolve, but the physical changes in the
neighborhood where its students are spending their childhood
already are obvious. Our experience clearly demonstrates how
much caring educators, a willing community, and empowered
families can achieve when they work together. (p 12)

Finally, this account by David Hartenbach, superintendent,
and his colleagues (1996) of the process by which the Aurora,
Colorado, public schools worked with staff members, parents,
and community leaders to develop—and sustain—a future-
oriented educational program.

For the past six years, Aurora Public School District, the fifth
largest in Colorado, has worked toward implementing an educational plan known as performance-based education. This plan
involves setting clear educational standards and having our students demonstrate that they have met these standards. In 1990,
Aurora schools involved thousands of staff, parents, and community stakeholders in a strategic learning process and adopted a
mission "to develop lifelong learners who value themselves, con-
tribute to their community, and succeed in a changing world."

The school system adopted five learner outcomes that require
students to be self-directed learners, collaborative workers,
complex thinkers, community contributors, and quality produc-
ers. These learner characteristics focus on the skills for successful learning both in and out of the classroom. Integral to
our educational vision are content standards that define what
students should know and be able to do at graduation and at
benchmarks along the way.

In addition, parents and staff worked side by side to develop graduation expectations that identify performances, products, or other measures required of graduates; and content areas and content standards required for graduation. The role of learner outcomes in the curriculum generated a great deal of debate. Some questioned the ability to accurately measure some learner outcomes. Others feared content would be diminished as a result of the emphasis on learner outcomes.

After much dialogue, parents, staff, and community members came to a consensus that teachers should model and teach learner outcomes, but that learner outcomes should not be a part of graduation requirements. It is significant that stakeholders reached consensus on learner outcomes, content standards, and graduation requirements, and that the district was willing to listen and respond—an example of genuine empowerment. (p. 52)

Aurora's story illustrates many aspects of a learning organization, including the use of processes for gathering information in a way appropriate to the district's purposes, having challenging but achievable goals, and modifying plans in response to feedback. Most of all it shows the quintessential characteristic of organizations that learn, which is to be fully and authentically engaged with the broader community, offering leadership but responding intelligently to social, economic, and political conditions. In today's world, each school must be a learning organization.

■    ■    ■

# References

# Sources of Knowledge About Learning

Alexander, P.A., and P.K. Murphy. (1998). "How Students Learn: Reform-
ing Schools Through Learner-Centered Education." In *Issues in
School Reform: A Sampler of Psychological Perspectives on Learner-
Centered Schools.*, edited by N. Lambert and B.L. McCombs. Washington, D.C.: APA Books.

American Psychological Association. (November 1997). "Learner-Centered Psychological Principles: A Framework for School Reform
and Redesign." Prepared by the Learner-Centered Principles Work
Group of the American Psychological Association's Board of Educational Affairs. Available from APA, 750 First Street, NE, Washington, D.C. 20002-4242. Also at http://www.apa.org/ed/lcp.html/ .

Caine, R.N., and G. Caine. (1997). *Education on the Edge of Possibility.* Alexandria, Va.: Association for Supervision and Curriculum Development.

Institute for Research on Learning. (n.d.). "Principles of Learning: Challenging Fundamental Assumptions." Menlo Park, Calif.: Author.

Leinhardt, G. (1992). "What Research on Learning Tells Us About Teaching." *Educational Leadership* 49, 7 (April): 20–25.

Leithwood, K., L. Leonard, and L. Sharrartt. (January 1997). "Conditions
Fostering Organizational Learning in Schools." Paper presented at
the annual meeting of the International Congress on School Effectiveness and Improvement, Memphis, Tenn.

Resnick, L. (1987). "Learning in School and Out." *Educational Researcher*
16, 4 (December): 13–20.

Sarason, S. (1997). *How Schools Might Be Governed and Why.* New York:
Teachers College Press.

Scottish Consultative Council on the Curriculum (Scottish CCC). (1996).
*Teaching for Effective Learning: A Paper for Discussion and Develop-
ment.* Dundee, Scotland: Author.

Senge, P.M. (1990). *The Fifth Discipline.* New York: Doubleday Currency.

Wenger, E. (1998). *Communities of Practice: Learning, Meaning, and Iden-
tity.* Cambridge: Cambridge University Press.

## Examples from Educational Leadership

Abernethy, P.E., and R.W. Serfass. (1992). "One District's Quality Improvement Story." *Educational Leadership* 50, 3 (November): 14–17.

Ackerman, R., P. Maslin-Ostrowski, and C. Christensen. (1996). "Case Stories: Telling Tales About School." *Educational Leadership* 53, 6 (March): 21–23.

Bradsher, M., and L. Hagan. (1995). "The Kids Network: Student-Scientists Pool Resources." *Educational Leadership* 53, 2 (October): 38–43.

Brandt, R. (1994a). "On Making Sense: A Conversation with Magdalene Lampert." *Educational Leadership* 51, 5 (February): 26–30.

Brandt, R. (1994b). "On Creating an Environment Where All Students Learn: A Conversation with Al Mamary." *Educational Leadership* 51, 6 (March): 24–28.

Brandt, R. (1996). "On a New Direction for Teacher Evaluation: A Conversation with Tom McGreal." *Educational Leadership* 53, 6 (March): 30–33.

Calfee, R.C., and C. Wadleigh. (1992). "How Project READ Builds Inquiring Schools." *Educational Leadership* 50, 1 (September): 28–32.

Castner, K., L. Costella, and S. Hess. (1993). "Moving from Seat Time to Mastery: One District's System." *Educational Leadership* 51, 1 (September): 45–50.

Collopy, R.B., and T. Green. (1995). "Using Motivational Theory with At-Risk Children." *Educational Leadership* 53, 1 (September): 37–40.

Corbett, A.H., S.W. Golder, and J. Hoffman. (1996). "A District's Response to Sexual Harassment." *Educational Leadership* 53, 8 (May): 69–71.

Cuozzo, C. (1996–97). "What Do Lepidopterists Do?" *Educational Leadership* 54, 4 (December/January): 34–37.

Daniels, H. (1996). "The Best Practice Project: Building Parent Partnerships in Chicago." *Educational Leadership* 53, 7 (April): 38–43.

Elliott, T.J. (1993). "Back in the Classroom." *Educational Leadership* 51, 2 (October): 28–30.

Farlow, L. (1996). "A Quartet of Success Stories: How to Make Inclusion Work." *Educational Leadership* 53, 5 (February): 51–55.

Fink, S. (1992). "How We Restructured Our Categorical Programs." *Educational Leadership* 50, 2 (October): 42–43.

Fowler, R.C., and K.K. Corley. (1996). "Linking Families, Building Community." *Educational Leadership* 53, 7 (April): 24–26.

Freiberg, H. J. (1996). "From Tourists to Citizens in the Classroom." *Educational Leadership* 54, 1 (September): 32–33.

Gersten, R. (1996). "The Double Demands of Teaching English Language Learners." *Educational Leadership* 53, 5 (February): 18–22.

Gross, S.J. (1996). "Creating a Learner's Bill of Rights—Vermont's Town Meeting Approach." *Educational Leadership* 53, 7 (April): 50–53.

Hartenbach, D.L., J. Ott, and S. Clark. (1996). "Performance-Based Education in Aurora." *Educational Leadership* 54, 4 (December): 51–55.

Hatch, T. (1997). "Getting Specific About Multiple Intelligences." *Educational Leadership* 54, 6 (March): 26–29.

Heckman, P.E., C.B. Confer, and D.C. Hakim. (1994). "Planting Seeds: Understanding Through Investigation." *Educational Leadership* 51, 5 (February): 36–39.

Herdman, P. (1994). "When the Wilderness Becomes a Classroom." *Educational Leadership* 52, 3 (November): 15–19.

Keller, B. (1995). "Accelerated Schools: Hands-On Learning in a Unified Community." *Educational Leadership* 52, 5 (February): 10–13.

Kessler, R. (1992). "Shared Decision Making Works!" *Educational Leadership* 50, 1 (September): 36–38.

Kirby-Lipton, K., N. Lyle, and S. White. (1996). "When Parents and Teachers Create Writing Standards." *Educational Leadership* 54, 4 (December): 30–32.

Koski, M. (1993). "Change—From the Grassroots Up." *Educational Leadership* 51, 1 (September): 51–52.

Lantieri, L., and J. Patti. (1996). "The Road to Peace in Our Schools." *Educational Leadership* 54, 1 (September): 28–31.

Lubetkin, M.T. (1996). "How Teamwork Transformed a Neighborhood." *Educational Leadership* 53, 7 (April): 10–12.

Marshall, S.P., and C. Hatcher. (1996). "Promoting Career Development Through CADRE." *Educational Leadership* 53, 6 (March): 42–46.

McFaden, D., and B. Nelson. (1995). "A Refuge for Real-World Learning." *Educational Leadership* 52, 8 (May): 11–13.

McLaughlin, M.W. (1992). "How District Communities Do and Do Not Foster Teacher Pride." *Educational Leadership* 50, 1 (September): 33–35.

Meadows, B.J., V. Shaw-Taylor, and F. Wilson. (1993). "Through the Eyes of Parents." *Educational Leadership* 51, 2 (October): 31–34.

Meyer, M.R., M.L. Delagardelle, and J.A. Middleton. (1996). "Addressing Parents' Concerns Over Curriculum Reform." *Educational Leadership* 53, 7 (April): 54–57.

Miller, P., K. Shambaugh, C. Robinson, and J. Wimberly. (1995). "Applied Learning for Middle Schoolers." *Educational Leadership* 52, 8 (May): 22–25.

Murphy, M., and A. Miller. (1996). "Incentives Pay Off in Technological Literacy." *Educational Leadership* 53, 6 (March): 54–56.

Perkins, D., and T. Blythe. (1994). "Putting Understanding Up Front." *Educational Leadership* 51, 5 (February): 4–7.

Prescott, C., B. Rinard, J. Cockerill, and N. Baker. (1996). "Science Through Workplace Lenses." *Educational Leadership* 53, 8 (May): 10–13.

Ramirez-Smith, C. (1995). "Stopping the Cycle of Failure: The Comer Model." *Educational Leadership* 52, 5 (February): 14–19.

Rugen, L., and S. Hartl. (1994). "The Lessons of Learning Expeditions." *Educational Leadership* 52, 3 (November): 20–23.

Sahakian, P., and J. Stockton. (1996). "Opening Doors: Teacher-Guided Observations." *Educational Leadership* 53, 6 (March): 50–53.

Scarr, L.E. (1992). "Using Self-Regulating Work Teams." *Educational Leadership* 50, 3 (November): 68–70.

Smith, K. (1993). "Becoming the 'Guide on the Side.'" *Educational Leadership* 51, 2 (October): 35–37.

Thompson, S. (1995). "The Community as Classroom." *Educational Leadership* 52, 8 (May): 17–20.

Vondra, J. (1996). "Resolving Conflicts Over Values." *Educational Leadership* 53, 7 (April): 76–79.

Wade, R. (1997). "Lifting a School's Spirit." *Educational Leadership* 54, 8 (May): 34–36.

Wagner, T. (1997). "The New Village Commons—Improving Schools Together." *Educational Leadership* 54, 5 (February): 25–28.

Weissberg, R.P., T.P. Shriver, S. Bose, and K. DeFalco. (1997). "Creating a Districtwide Social Development Project." *Educational Leadership* 54, 8 (May): 37–39.

Woehrle, T. (1993). "Growing Up Responsible." *Educational Leadership* 51, 3 (November): 40–43.

Wolk, S. (1994). "Project-Based Learning: Pursuits with a Purpose." *Educational Leadership* 52, 3 (November): 42–45.

Zorfass, J., and H. Copel. (1995). "The I-Search: Guiding Students Toward Relevant Research." *Educational Leadership* 53, 1 (September): 48–51.

## About the Author

Education writer and consultant Ron Brandt is the former editor of *Educational Leadership* and other publications of the Association for Supervision and Curriculum Development (ASCD).

During his tenure as editor of *Educational Leadership*, Brandt wrote more than 100 editorials and published "conversations" with more than 50 leading educators. In 1996, he was one of the first persons inducted into the EdPress Hall of Fame for his contributions to education publishing. He is author or coauthor of numerous publications including *Dimensions of Thinking, Dimensions of Learning*, and *The Language of Learning*, a glossary of education terminology published by ASCD in 1997.

Brandt began his career in Racine, Wisconsin, as a teacher of English. He has served as a junior high school principal in Racine, director of staff development in Minneapolis, Minnesota, associate superintendent in Lincoln, Nebraska, and staff member of a regional educational laboratory. In the 1960s, Brandt taught at a teacher training college in Nigeria, West Africa.

He can be reached at 1104 Woodcliff Dr., Alexandria, VA 22308-1058; telephone: (703) 765-4779; fax: (703) 765-8038; e-mail: ron.brandt@mci2000.com